FROG JOY

BETH GULLEY

FROG JOY

by Beth Gulley

Anamcara Press LLC

Published in 2024 by Anamcara Press LLC

Author © 2024 Beth Gulley
Book design by Maureen Carroll
Cover Illustration by Jane Blakeley
Georgia, Abril Text, and Minion Pro.
Printed in the United States of America.

Book Description: Dive into "Frog Joy," a collection of poems where Beth Gulley's verses paint everyday magic. From mulberry-stained fingers to a heart-pounding escape from floods, hear the chorus of frog calls serenading life's simple wonders.

ANAMCARA PRESS LLC
P.O. Box 442072, Lawrence, KS 66044
https://anamcara-press.com/

Ordering Information:
Quantity sales. Special discounts are available on quantity purchases by corporations, associations, and others. For details, contact the publisher at the address above.
Orders by U.S. trade bookstores and wholesalers. Please contact Ingram Distribution.

Gulley, Beth. Author
Frog Joy

POE024000 POETRY / Women Authors
POE005010 POETRY / American / General
POE023030 POETRY / Subjects & Themes / Animals & Nature

ISBN-13: 978-1-960462-24-4 (Paperback)
ISBN-13: 978-1-960462-25-1 (EBook)
ISBN-13: 978-1-960462-26-8 (Hardcover)

Library of Congress Control Number: 2023951567

"If what I say resonates with you,
it is merely because we are both branches
on the same tree."

—W.B. Yeats

Contents

PART V: Tuesday: Nothing To Report

ABOUT THE AUTHOR

DEDICATION—

For Jeremy, Israel, and Asher and for the Writing in the Garden friends.

PART I:
The Fighter Doesn't Dance Around

Amanda "Haiku" Nunes

The fighter
doesn't dance around.
She goes straight
for the takedown.
The fight is done
48 seconds
into round one.

Viewers are left
thinking "I paid
for this?" and
"I need to see
this fight
a few hundred
more times."

Announcers are
left speechless
and unprepared.
It's like reading Basho
for the first time.

Beth Gulley

Mandatory Training

Mandatory training
took her mind
to a safe space
where harassment
is reported,
cybercrime averted,
and privacy laws
upheld.

Next time her day
devolves into chaos—
like today when she
crashed into the dumpster
and smashed her rear window—
she will remember
to center herself
by meditating
on mandatory training.

Prey

Amid the empty crab shells,
feathers, and fish bones
on the rocky beach
at Mira Flores,
I remember I am prey.

I stick out on the rocks,
but after 42 years
I've done a better job
of not getting caught
than some.

Beth Gulley

There Was Not Enough Room
on the Postcard

There was not enough room on the postcard to write—

The truth is any city you are not in holds
no magic for me

My day starts when you bring the coffee and ends
when you turn out the lights

Since I've been gone it's been one long fuzzy Monday

even though the Facebook posts look sweet

so instead, I write

Hello from New Orleans

and hope you guess what I mean.

Mother's Concerns

My husband explains:
fathers don't care
about their son's coats.

Sons can tell
if they feel cold,
go to the closet,
and pull out a coat.

As long as coats exist
at the moment
sons feel cold,
then fathers don't worry.

The kind, the color, the size,
the judgement from teachers
when sons choose
not to wear coats,
these are mothers' concerns.

Beth Gulley

I Can't Cry on a Pink Cake

I can't cry on a pink cake,
says the tv lady.

She has conflated the pastry
with her mother's death
from breast cancer.

She makes an understated dish
topped with white chocolate flowers.

Her cake stands strong
like a woman in stage 4 who walks
Relay for Life for the last time.

Maps

What if darkness had come
and you were lost?

Maps bubble up
in my mind's eye.
Sometimes they appear
like fields from
an airplane window.
Other times they float
like a canoe
under a willow tree.

Maps shift and twist,
but they are always
on the horizon.
Like chess has rules,
my world has order,
connections, patterns.

I could never
get lost out there.
My internal compass
guides me home.

*Phrases in italics come from *The Sound of Music*
conversation between the Reverend Mother and
Maria at the beginning of the movie.

Beth Gulley

After So Much Netflix

Look up from the page.

You—hero of your own story.

Applaud yourself.

You've stopped binging tv

long enough

to find yourself

READING again.

Hurry. Look back down,

or you may never return.

On Talking to a Friend About Her Father's Stroke

She worries about her mother
driving to and fro
after dark, in spring snowstorms,
with the stress of her husband's stroke
to distract her.

She worries about her dog
sick after too much food—
an emotional response
to being boarded short notice.

She worries about her siblings
making snap decisions
an attempt to resolve
the new discomfort.

She's worried, but now
is the time other people
should shoulder some
of her concern and give her rest.

Beth Gulley

Chokehold

The heat sneaks in like cholesterol

and chokes out your life blood

in undetectable snippets.

Then all the sudden

you are walking

and you need to sit down

because you just can't breathe.

If only the sun would respond

to Lipitor or eating less bacon.

Cicadas

Your mom told me

cicadas were the voices

of people tormented in hell.

She also mentioned

she bought a new house

so she wouldn't have to worry

about who had died there.

It's a good thing

I was a skeptical teen

already rooted in my own beliefs

by the time she shared

her thoughts with me.

Otherwise, I doubt

I have been able to sleep

in your neighborhood

that summer.

Beth Gulley

Unscheduled Time

Rain caused

unexpected

change of plans.

Now I'm caught

between the cat

and the blanket

and the scary

possibilities

of unscheduled

time.

Call Before You Come

You caught my grammar

with its shoes off.

If you want me to put

my best foot forward,

call before you come.

PART II:
Frog Joy

Frog Joy

Here I am again,
spending the evening
parsing through frog calls,
trying to match
the chorus outside.

One call sounds like
two marbles knocking.
Another sounds like
fingers running along
the edge of a comb.

As I listen to the next one,
I forget the one before.
I lose hope of matching
the sound and the frog.

I open the door
and just listen
to the frog joy
in the damp night.

Beth Gulley

I Want Summer

I want summer cicada sounds

I want sweaty feet and itchy legs

I want hot sand and cold lake water

I want light to last late into the evening

I want freezie pops and fresh tomatoes

I want dollar drinks at Quick Trip

I want early morning dew smell and a soft pink sunrise

But more than anything,

I want to be five again

climbing in the Ozarks

with my dad until my legs get tired

and he lifts me on his shoulders

and carries me.

Micro Poems from the Community Garden July 2022

Birds chatter

Eavesdroppers

Don't know the code

Rose petals

Lose their pink

Refuse to fall

Dragonfly doesn't heed

Messages shouted

From a passing car

Baby rabbits in the hedge

Nine months after bunny prom

Beth Gulley

Birds Announce The Presence of Strangers

Birds announce the presence of strangers in the garden.

Chairs assist in our meditation by keeping the bugs from pouring over our legs.

Ice squeezes through our fingers as we return to the car to calm ourselves.

Weeds demonstrate their resilience. Berries refuse to shrivel in the heat.

Friends cajole as lunch calls. Its ring serves as a signal to go home.

July Micro Poem Collection

2 a.m. after too much coffee
Awake again all night
Wondering
> Why?

> Trail dust, spider webs
> still undisturbed, July sun
> too hot for horses

> The small strawberry
> tastes sour, seedy, better
> because I stole it

The thoughtless
celebrate noisily
whisky helps him sleep
stars emerge

> Too long summer days
> I quit
> in bed before sunset

Beth Gulley

No Snakes

No snakes
in the garden tonight

Just rabbit
and me

Washing hands
by the grape arbor

in the sunset

Without a Fence

My childhood backyard
went on forever

We would run and hide
in the base of a fir tree

We grazed on wild grapes
and stain our fingers
from low hanging mulberries

We were a gaggle
of semi unsupervised
children who could only watch
thirty minutes of tv
after school

We had to make our own world
without a fence
under a Kansas sky

PART III:
Tanka Journal
Kenya 2022

Tanka Journal
Kenya 2022

May 18

Heart attack mid air
Emergency stop, Boston
Pink late spring sunset
over the ocean, bonus
for all the well passengers

May 19

Seat leaner won't wake
for the dinner service so
food is hard to reach
She pays with my knees jabbing
though the rest of the long flight

May 20

The Warthog waddles
The Elephant minds it's child
Lion refuses to mate
Tonight at safari park
we sleep in tents with toilets

Beth Gulley

May 21

The Maasai introduce
two poison and three healing
plants for medicine
or war against a lion.
Take snaps for iNaturalist

May 22

The land welcomes you
back. Remember everything
started here in Eden
On a cellular level
you are beckoned to remain

May 23

In the kitchen we
drink tea, eat chapati, learn
Swahili, English
and Kalenjin while two cats
cry for scraps. Nico strains milk.

May 24

A small piece of chalk,
A skilled, knowledgeable, kind
teacher, and love are
really all one needs to get
quality education.

May 25
(Upon reading news of the Uvalde elementary school
shooting)

I hand him my phone.
Read it to yourself, I say.
There are kids in this
car that don't need the burden
of knowing kids die at school.

May 26

Six preschoolers and
their teacher play memory
on a low table.
Twenty sixth graders write poems,
stand to recite tongue twisters.

Beth Gulley

May 27

In a window seat
I see the river below,
skating by farmland
that cleverly knit itself
together along the banks.

PART IV:
Your Grace Is Enough

I'm Racing the Maris Des Cygnes

I'm racing the Marais Des Cygnes
as it ambles towards flood stage

I should know better,
trust the weather experts

But my own best judgment
tells me the trail I'm on was built
for the railroad so chances are good
the water won't reach this high.

Regardless, I run a little faster
as the water slowly rises below me.

Meanwhile Nana is in the hospital
for the third time in so many weeks.

She is racing the infection
that wanders from the kidneys
to the stomach to the lungs.

She is there to listen
to the medical experts.

Her own best judgment

tells her this fight
is one all of us eventually lose.

Regardless, she fights a little harder,
hangs on a little while more.

Beth Gulley

Jesus Has Meth Teeth (Matthew 25:40)

Jesus has meth teeth
and fading pink hair.
She needs eleven dollars
and eight cents
to cover the Z-Trip
to her mother's house.
I buy her a drink
and give her the change.
It's just over what she
asked for.
The whole exchange
is subtle, ordinary, humbling.

I haven't seen Jesus
since he was lost
on his first day
at a new school,
or maybe the day
he was trying to stay
out of the rain
as he picked up
recycled cans.
As always,
I'm grateful for the chance
to be of service.
This time at a random
Quick Trip
on a Saturday.

For Father's Day

Sixteen things I remember about my dad...

He kept caramels in his guayabera pocket
to hand out to kids after church.

He swam the butterfly and practiced
at the pool near Atami Beach.

He could type really fast because he was the only kid in
his high school who couldn't sing, so he took three years
of typing while everyone else was in choir.

He spoke Spanish with a British accent.

He had a ham radio operator's license, and he knew
Morse code from his days in the army.

He liked to put ketchup on food.

He was good at telling stories and often began his ser-
mons with them.

He played basketball on a rec league.

He gave out the white tornado award when he hosted
church camp.

He would put on a red hat and pretend to be his brother
Fred. Uncle Fred often brought the last birthday present.

He made up a song that supposedly Olivia was playing

when she cleaned the piano—sucío, sucio, muy sucio.

He helped me write to prospective colleges and get admissions information sent to me in Paraguay.

He taught me how to study by helping me prepare for tests in Mr. Cronin's history class.

My dad liked to visit historic places. Our last vacation was to the Missions in Paraguay.

He liked to go on nature hikes. When I was really little, he would carry me on his shoulders while we walked.

He loved God, my mom, and tried to love everyone else too. He was his authentic self all the time.

He died of pneumonia a few months after he started teaching me to drive. It's been thirty-two years since I've seen him. The empty space he left has clouded over, but his love and faith sustain me still.

While on a tour of the Church that houses Pizzaro's Bones

Pelicans--

She explained

in very clear Spanish--

symbolize Christ

because they peck

their chests

until they bleed

to feed their young

when other food

cannot be found.

Then she leads us

beneath the altar

to see the bones

of children

"blessed" to rest

so near to God.

My mothering heart

wanted to cover the tomb

with stones, take them

Beth Gulley

out of public view.

The heart of God

is like a hen with her chicks.

He shelters us under his wings

He doesn't charge admission

to show our suffering

to the Angels.

Post Victory Pain

After you win

and the talk of your victory

skitters off like fog in midday sun

you are left with an empty space

that WANT used to fill.

You'll have to imagine

something else to need.

Beth Gulley

January 1, 2022

A tree branch rests

on a power line—

precarious start

to the New Year.

Home Blessing 2022

May our home
be full of warmth
and laughter.

Protect us from
all unreasonableness.

Keep us from those
who would sit in our spots
or change our routines.

Help us always
have Cheez-its
and Dr Pepper.

May joy
and peace prevail.

In the name of our Lord
we pray. Amen.

Beth Gulley

All the Room in the World

One summer
we pitched a tent
outside my grandparents
house in the Sandhills

We were 100 yards
from the outhouse—
a two-seater

All seven aunts
and uncles
with spouses
and kids
slept inside

A three bedroom
with one bathroom.

In our Coleman tent
we had all the room
in the world.

Mile 17

Mile 17
of my first
Marine corps
Marathon
my legs cramped
my lungs burned

I had started
too fast
fallen behind
lost myself
in tension

My hair so salty
I could quit,
I ran past
the Jesus radio
station
playing Your
Grace Is Enough.

It broke something
loose.
I pushed
through the wall.
I found
a release
I didn't know
I needed.

Beth Gulley

Moving Target

I thought it was funny

at the time, telling

a surprised Chinese girl

and graduate student

from Burundi

about the night

I bought a gun

at a bible study.

In retrospect,

after the secret

relationship

between the church

and the NRA

was revealed

though the magic

of MAGA,

I'm no longer laughing.

Seeds

She carried the little seed

since after Memorial Day

but it started to sprout

on the 4th of July

when she realized

her college boys

would be driving home

at night and through

no fault of their own

potentially not make it

to their driveways.

The thorny little start

of a thought branched

as she remembered

on Memorial Day

Megan was here

and then she wasn't.

PART V:
Tuesday: Nothing To Report

Bunnies

I don't know

what magical algorithm

determined

I needed to see

folksy drawings

of bunny rabbits,

but they pegged me

exactly right.

I hope next

they find me

photos of fairy gardens.

Beth Gulley

There Will Be Silence While You Wait

There will be silence
while you wait. Don't fill it with
anxious empty thoughts.

Not every day flows
with important information.
Some days just are.

When you looked again,
a water stain slice of moon
peers behind a cloud.

A hailstorm startles
drivers. God, it seems, wants them
to turn and go home.

One more set to win
all the marbles. Don't walk out
before it's finished.

A Tooth Surface Color Code Chart

A Tooth Surface Color Code Chart

hangs on the wall behind the poet.

The teeth look like a small army

of robot people with multicolor heads.

The robot people seem to listen

attentively as though receiving instructions.

The poet continues, but I've lost the thread.

The teeth robots have chewed my focus.

Beth Gulley

The Constant Dripping

Handle jiggling

won't stop the toilet running

wasting fresh water

others could drink or wash in.

Guilt, the constant dripping sound.

The Succulents

The succulents
extend their vacation
on the patio.

The calendar
and the weather app
concur it's ok.

The house plants
hope to stake a claim
on their summer home.

For now, though,
they maintain a lease
on the dresser.

Beth Gulley

Solidarity

(For the 2008 Jayhawks)

On a flight home
from a conference
I pay to get the game
on the screen in front of me.

I can hear the other passengers
hold their breath, then exhale
as our home team makes a basket.

We land at half time.
We file out quickly
into the crisp March air
to cross our fingers
and say our prayers
and hope our home team
to another shot
at the National title.

In the Psychic Calendar

In the psychic calendar

she carries in her mind

she flipped her imaginary

pencil to the eraser side

and cleared the rest of the box

marked "today."

Imaginary eraser dust

brushed by with her real breath

and the rush of her muscles

unclenching

Beth Gulley

Tuesday

Nothing to report.

I squeeze a teddy bear

while lounging on the couch

watching basketball.

The cat at my feet

squeaks when disturbed

from her evening nap spot.

No worries, no regrets

No extraordinary happenings.

Nothing new tonight.

Erasure

She came to rely
on digital erasers.

Foiled by a photo
she couldn't remove,

She yearned for her
school days liquid paper.

Instead, she hid her work
in the blue recycle bin.

Giving up had become
preferable to owning up.

Invisibility came knocking,
and he brought a baseball bat.

Beth Gulley

In the classroom

Different shades of silence

shake out like salt, sugar, or

a mailbox full of ants

Doing Nothing

I spend the evening

doing nothing of consequence.

I look at photos of friends

who spend the day sitting

on the floor of the museum/

train station/ main street.

I think my way of doing nothing

is boring.

Beth Gulley

Product Placement Pens

Product placement pens

pile up at the bottom

of my purse.

I pull them out

in insecure moments

to feel the ad world

pushing for me.

I Can't Face The Dark

I can't face the dark clouds
to eat lunch alone at home
without you who are flying to Detroit

So I eat alone in my
windowless office
appeased by the illusion

of work to do on a toxic
screen under fluorescent
bulbs with the hum of others

filling in the background

Beth Gulley

Bike Ride

A black number 128
smudged with bike grease
fades into her leg

She pulls her bike out
for a post triathlon
Sunday ride with Jane

The winding blacktop path
and the dense trees
seem a real version
of the fake trail
on the stationary bike screen
at the gym

She becomes so lost
in the un-reality
she can't remember
what a red light means
and almost coasts into a car

Rainbows

Brown eyes

starve for light.

Blue eyes

wish it away.

Rainbows,

uniters that they are,

slide light

through dark,

let us sit together.

Beth Gulley

Lucky Number 7

Affirmation poked through
the golden crumble
of her fortune cookie.

You are more intelligent
than you give yourself credit
lucky number 7.

She taped it
to the inside of her math book
pretending it was meant for her.

A Dew Drop On a Spider Web

(For 9th Grade English)

I don't like cliche poems
like dew drops on a spider web
are like diamonds
my classmate said.

I nodded
as I placed my hand
over my 9th grade English
notebook.

The dew drops
from the poem I wrote
practically wound themselves
around my wrist--

A diamond bracelet
of cliches.

Beth Gulley

A Wild Fray of Threads

We still wear Kenya dust
on our feet as we climb
the hill to Berkeley

wading through puddles
of homeless people
to reach the pinnacle
of human creativity.

There we catch
a speed round of chess
and a storefront game
of guess which celebrity
grew from this baby picture.

The world is a wild fray
of threads.
Together we snatch a few
to weave a nest.

The Year of the Dog

The year you went to Thailand
was the year of the dog.

We text you the story of

the tiny white dog
that wandered into
our drunk friend's bed
one night when he left
his door open.

We took the dog home
as a patch for
the puncture wound
your absence poked
into our family.

The little dog
didn't fix everything.
But he helped.

ACKNOWLEDGEMENTS

Thank you to the following for publishing poems from this collection:

"Cicadas." Thorny Locust, 2023.
"Amanda 'Haiku' Nunes." The Write Bridge, No. 5, Summer 2023.
"Mandatory Training." Kansas Speaks Out: Poems in the age of Me, Too. An Actual Kansas Press, 2022.
"Call Before You Come," "Post Victory Pain," 365 Days Poem Anthology Volume 4, 2022.
"I'm Racing the Maris Des Cynes," Voices from the Writers Place Audio Book, 2023.
"Jesus Has Meth Teeth (Matthew 25:40)," Dragonfly, 2022.
"The Year of the Dog," Kansas City Voices, 2023.

Furthermore, thank you to all those who joined me at Writing in the Garden/Park events. It was a blessing to write alongside you. Many of these poems were born during one of these events.
Thank you to the 365 Poems Facebook group, and to the Collaborators.
Finally, thank you to Jeremy Gulley for always being my first audience and best editor.